Grime, Crime and Convicts

A Trip into the Past

Jill McDougall

Illustrations by Julia Castaño

Grime, Crime and Convicts: A Trip into the Past

Text: Jill McDougall
Publishers: Tania Mazzeo and Eliza Webb
Series consultant: Amanda Sutera
  Hands on Heads Consulting
Editor: Laken Ballinger
Project editor: Annabel Smith
Designer: Leigh Ashforth
Project designer: Danielle Maccarone
Permissions researcher: Catherine Kerstjens
Production controller: Renee Tome

Acknowledgements
We would like to thank the following for permission to reproduce
copyright material:

Front cover, pp. 3–6, 10, 13, 14, 17–22, back cover: Julia Castaño ©
Cengage Learning Australia; pp. 1, 11: Alamy Stock Photo/Heritage Image
Partnership Ltd; p. 7: Alamy Stock Photo/PRISMA ARCHIVO; p. 8 (top):
Getty Images/Stock Montage, (bottom): Getty Images/Print Collector; p. 9
(top): Getty Images/Bildagentur-online, (bottom): Alamy Stock
Photo/Florilegius; p. 12: Alamy Stock Photo/IanDagnall Computing; p. 15
(top): Shutterstock.com/ArliftAtoz2205, (bottom): Alamy Stock
Photo/Chronicle; p. 16: Museum of Sydney Collection, Museums of
History NSW. Model © Lynne and Laurie Hadley. Photo © Jamie North.

Every effort has been made to trace and acknowledge copyright.
However, if any infringement has occurred, the publishers tender their
apologies and invite the copyright holders to contact them.

NovaStar

ISBN 978 0 17 033430 3

Cengage Learning Australia
Level 5, 80 Dorcas Street
Southbank VIC 3006 Australia
Phone: 1300 790 853
Email: aust.nelsonprimary@cengage.com

For learning solutions, visit cengage.com.au

Printed in China by 1010 Printing International Ltd
1 2 3 4 5 6 7 28 27 26 25 24

*Nelson acknowledges the Traditional Owners and Custodians
of the lands of all First Nations Peoples. We pay respect
to Elders past and present, and extend that respect to
all First Nations Peoples today.*

Contents

London, England, 1787

Here you are, on a street in the city of London, England, during the year 1787. It's noisy and crowded and a bit smelly.

Okay, it's *very* smelly. Piles of horse **dung** are scattered over the **cobblestones**, and what's that ahead? It looks like a slimy old cabbage someone has tossed out of a window. Wait a minute ... it *is* a slimy old cabbage! After all, there's no such thing as rubbish collection in London in 1787.

You hurry past a row of houses in a **slum**, where broken windows are blocked with rags that have been stuffed into the open spaces. Children huddle on doorsteps, looking cold and hungry.

Then … *squeak!* Something scurries across your foot. A rat! And if that isn't bad enough, what's that awful stink? *Pew!* It's coming from a deep hole at the end of the road called a "cesspit".

A cesspit? Yes! It's an outdoor toilet that's shared by everyone who lives nearby.

You shudder and hurry away.

It's a Fact!

In London in the 1700s, human **waste**, dead animals and rubbish were all thrown into the streets or the river.

As you continue your journey through London, you notice that it's hard to breathe. The air is thick with smoke that belches from the factory chimneys. You peer inside the dirty windows of one of these factories, and you see people hard at work on noisy machines. Some of these workers are even small children.

Children? Can this be true? Yes!

In the late 1700s, children as young as four years old worked in factories to help feed their families.

* They worked six days a week, usually from 6 am to 6 pm.

* Sometimes, they were beaten for whistling, singing or even *talking*!

* Some of these children were **orphans** who worked for food and a place to sleep.

* Accidents were common, and many children died.

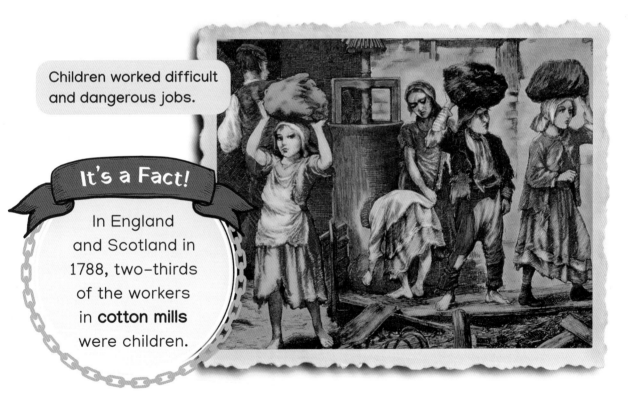

Children worked difficult and dangerous jobs.

It's a Fact!

In England and Scotland in 1788, two-thirds of the workers in **cotton mills** were children.

You may be thinking, what led to these terrible conditions? Surely life in England wasn't always like this?

No, not at all!

From Country to City

Before factories were built, most **British** people lived in the countryside and made everything they needed by hand. However, in the 1700s, new machines were invented that could make products a lot faster. For example, the new spinning machine could spin cotton eight times faster than the spinning wheels people used in their homes.

A spinning wheel is a wooden machine people used to make thread from wool.

It's a Fact!

In Britain, the invention of new machines led to changes in farming, transport and **industry**. This time period, from around 1750 to 1840, is called "the Industrial Revolution".

New steam-powered spinning machines could make thread much faster than a single spinning wheel.

Many families got food from public soup kitchens, which were very crowded.

Huge factories were built as places to set up these new machines. People living in the country moved to London or other cities to work in the factories. They didn't just move in the hundreds or the thousands – they moved in the *hundreds of thousands*.

At that time, cities like London were not built for large **populations**. There were not enough houses, so families had to share overcrowded rooms that had no toilets or anywhere to wash. As you can imagine, diseases spread quickly.

Thomas Hudson was a well-known London beggar who wore a rug around his shoulders.

To make matters worse, not everyone could find work. Many people were starving. What could they do to survive? Some became beggars in the street, and others stole whatever they could find.

Crime and Punishment

As you roam London's overcrowded streets, beware! There are pickpockets about.

Pickpockets? Yes, that's exactly what they do – they are thieves who can pick anything of value out of people's pockets. Sometimes, they even wear fancy clothes to fool their victims.

The grand houses of the rich are targets for thieves, too. And, in the British countryside, robbers **hold up** horse-drawn carriages as they transport people from one place to another.

a pickpocket in action

A robber holds up a rich person's carriage.

You might ask, what happened to criminals who were caught? Well, punishments at this time were harsh, because the people in charge believed that was the best way to stop people committing crimes. For example, in 1787:

* A pickpocket could be flogged, or beaten, in the street.
* A **poacher** could be sentenced to death for hunting a rabbit.
* A child could be sent to prison for stealing a loaf of bread.

You won't be surprised to hear that the British prisons were soon full. To solve this problem, some of the prisoners were held inside old ships called "hulks". Soon, the hulks were full, too.

The British government needed to find somewhere else to send prisoners – known as convicts.

Hulks were **moored** in rivers and harbours, and convicts were often brought ashore to work.

The Perfect Place

Meanwhile, an explorer named Captain James Cook had brought news of an unknown land on the other side of the world. The British called this land New South Wales, and the government decided it would be the perfect place to send convicts.

The British government ignored the fact that the land was already occupied, or lived in. They were determined to start a new **colony** that would be owned by Britain. And who would build this colony? Convicts!

But how did the convicts get to this faraway land? Let's put you in the picture ...

It's a Fact!

Captain Cook thought he discovered a new land, but it had been occupied for more than 65 000 years by **First Nations** peoples.

Captain Cook was an explorer, and he drew maps of the lands he visited.

You're standing outside a large prison in London, and you notice a horse-drawn cart rumbling out of the prison gates. The cart is crammed with people, and you see the terrified faces of men, women and, yes, even children. The convicts are tied together with chains and surrounded by guards.

Someone tells you that these convicts are being transported to New South Wales. The cart will carry them along bumpy roads for 250 kilometres to the **port** of Portsmouth. There, a fleet of ships is waiting to carry them across the ocean to the other side of the world.

It's a Fact!

"Transportation" was a form of punishment given to convicts. Those sentenced to transportation could be sent to a distant place for 7 years, 14 years or for life!

The First Fleet

On 13 May 1787, eleven ships set sail from Portsmouth, England, under the **command** of Captain Arthur Phillip. The ships were headed for Botany Bay, and they came to be known as the First Fleet. They travelled more than 24 000 kilometres with 1400 people on board. No fleet of ships had ever carried so many people so far.

The ships were heavily loaded with anything that might be needed in the new colony. This included furniture, seeds, wagons and wheelbarrows. There were even 5000 bricks and 747 000 nails on board!

Map of the First Fleet's Journey

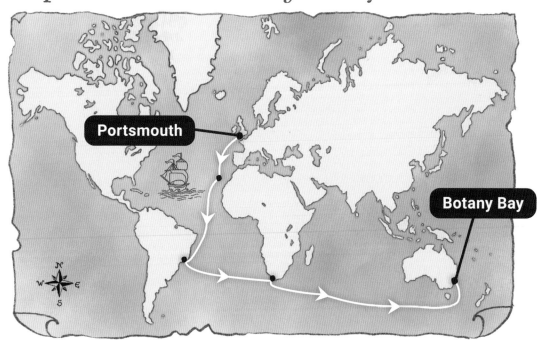

Six ships in the First Fleet had convicts on board.
Three of the convicts were younger than 14 years old.
What crimes did these children commit?

- John Hudson broke into a house
  and stole clothes and a gun.
  He was 8 years old when he first
  went to prison.

- Elizabeth Hayward stole some
  clothes and tried to sell them.
  She was about 13 years old
  when she was found guilty.

- George Youngson broke into
  a house and stole money.
  He was about 12 when he was
  sent to prison.

A statue in Sydney, Australia,
lists the names of everyone
who travelled on the First Fleet.

The First Fleet entered Botany Bay in
New South Wales on 20 January 1788.

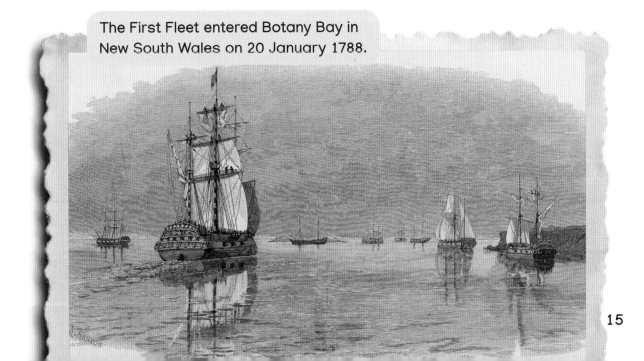

The Convict Transport Ships

Name of Ship	Length of Ship	Number of Convicts	Fast Fact
Charlotte	32 metres	92–94 men 29 women	Around 20 convicts on board had been in a famous **mutiny**.
Friendship	23 metres	72 men 21 women	John Hudson (the youngest convict) was transported on this ship.
Alexander	35 metres	195 men	Around 15 convicts on this ship died of disease.
Prince of Wales	31 metres	49 women 2 men	This ship had outbreaks of rats, fleas and lice.
Lady Penrhyn	31.5 metres	101 women	This was the slowest ship in the First Fleet.
Scarborough	34 metres	208 men	This was the only ship to transport convicts to New South Wales on two different voyages.

It's a Fact!

Most convicts on the First Fleet were British, but some were American and French, and some were from Africa.

The voyage of the First Fleet lasted 252 days. During this time, the passengers suffered through raging storms, sweltering heat and freezing cold.

Imagine you have been caught stealing, and your punishment is transportation to New South Wales.

You're crammed into a dark space in the lower part of the ship, known as the hold. Above you is a small **hatch** that leads to the **deck**. Soon, the hatch will be closed and locked to make sure you and the other convicts don't escape.

You've never been on a ship before, and you're terrified. How will you survive the long voyage to a strange new land?

From somewhere up above comes the sound of the captain shouting orders to the crew, and you're startled by the noise of sails flapping violently in the wind. Then, the ship gives a lurch. You're on your way!

Hang on tight! The ship is swaying from side to side, and suddenly your stomach heaves. You can tell from the groans and smells around you that you're not the only one who is seasick.

It's crowded here in the hold, and some of the convicts are covered in dirt, sores and even lice! It's clear that no one had a proper wash for months. After all, every convict was in a prison of some sort before boarding.

You decide to take a look around. *Ouch!* You hit your head! The roof is so low only small children can stand up straight. No wonder everyone is stooped over.

Hungry? Twice a day, buckets of soup or stew are lowered into the hold by a rope, and you can fill a metal cup from the bucket. It may not seem like much food, but for some of the convicts, this is the first time in their lives they have eaten regular meals.

When it's time for bed, you lie on a large shelf fitted in the side of the ship. At least there's a thin mattress to sleep on! The bad news? You need to share your mattress with two or three others.

When wild storms batter the ship, seawater rushes down the hatch and soaks the bedding. Look out! The toilet bucket is spilling its contents into the swirling water below your feet. *Eww!*

In fine weather, the convicts on the ship are allowed up on deck to scrub their filthy clothes and dry out their mattress. It's a relief to breathe fresh, clean air.

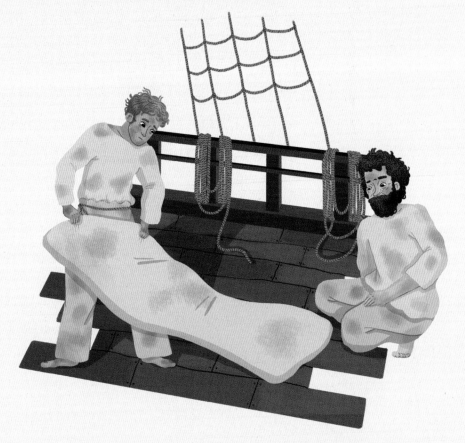

During the long voyage, the ships call in at three different ports to take on fresh food and water. At one port, Captain Phillip buys sacks of **tapioca**, and some of the convicts make clothes out of the empty bags.

The ships stay in Cape Town, South Africa, for a month while cows, pigs and other animals are brought on board for the new colony. For that entire month, you're locked below decks in the sweltering stink.

Arrival

Finally, on 19 January 1788, the **lookouts** on the First Fleet sight the coast of New South Wales. You're almost there!

When you're allowed to climb to the upper deck, you catch your first sight of this new land. Once the sailors land on the shore, they busily cut down trees and put up tents. At the edge of a clearing, the British flag flutters in the breeze. Captain Phillip has claimed possession of the land.

Then, you see something in the distance. On a rocky ridge, a group of people stand silently watching.

Your hands grasp the ship's rail as you gaze at the scene, and you wonder ... *what does the future hold*?

Glossary

British (*adjective*) — from the island of Britain (including England, Scotland and Wales) or Northern Ireland

cobblestones (*noun*) — small, rounded stones that are used for making streets

colony (*noun*) — a country or area under the control of a more powerful country that is often far away

command (*noun*) — control or authority

cotton mills (*noun*) — buildings with machinery for spinning cotton

deck (*noun*) — the floor of a ship

dung (*noun*) — solid droppings from large animals

First Nations peoples (*noun*) — the first peoples living in an area

hatch (*noun*) — a door cut into the deck of a ship

hold up (*verb*) — to rob someone of the money they're carrying by threatening them

industry (*noun*) — the making of products, usually in a factory

lookouts (*noun*) — people on a ship who keep watch for danger or signs of land

moored (*verb*) — held in place with ropes or an anchor

mutiny (*noun*) — when sailors on a ship take control from the person in charge

orphans (*noun*) — children whose parents have died

poacher (*noun*) — a person who breaks the law by hunting and stealing animals

populations (*noun*) — numbers of people living in certain places

port (*noun*) — a city or town where ships can stop

slum (*noun*) — an area of a city that is in poor condition

tapioca (*noun*) — hard white grains made from the root of a plant

waste (*noun*) — things that need to be thrown away

Index